words previously unspoken

J Gallops

Writers Club Press

San Jose New York Lincoln Shanghai

Published by Writers Club Press
an imprint of iUniverse.com, Inc.

For information address:
iUniverse.com, Inc.
620 North 48th Street
Suite 201
Lincoln, NE 68504-3467
www.iuniverse.com

ISBN: 0-595-09617-4

Printed in the United States of America

dedicated

Miranda

Linsey

Loretta

Karen

Tres

Judson

Denny

Christina

Worm

and Rachel

Acknowledgements

Walter F. Spara, for teaching me how to write poetry. Hope you enjoy your retirement.

"Those that are Dedicated," ...what can I say? Thanks for everything. I don't think I would ever have finished this if it were not for you guys.

God the Father, the Son, and the Holy Spirit, for giving me the inspiration, creativity, and time.

Contents

210 Grimsley Street

I can see it from here.

At times I think it lonely:
a double-story mansion
standing like it was a graveyard
painted in cobwebs.

The windows are cracked
around the house.

The wood is splintered out
as sharp as needles:
a last protection perhaps
against all who would approach.

I remember of
the Egyptian pyramids
being built
so long ago,

to be the overseeing tombs
for dead pharaohs.

But no one dead is here.
Only this collapsing building,
falling by its own corpse-like hands
keeping all the fatal wounds open,
falling to the ground.

I wonder if those pyramids
ever had a speared fence around them,
ever had a first line of defense,
attempting to protect them so well?
Or did that tribe just fall down,
buried in the sand by similar vines
sweeping to strangle this gate
to pieces?

The roof is one
reaching up like a knife
to scrape away
all the colors of the sky.

Yet as filthy as this house is,
no one will ever uproot this tomb,
no one will ever really see
the torn screen door,
the rock-shattered walls,

the old screeching women
always standing in the clear
with those silent staring birds.

Second Apocalypse

My hands are dirty,
digging.

I never thought
I would have to do so much
for my mother's grave.
Reaching into the ground
without a shovel,
taking out handfuls.

Like the king's dead jester,
all the bones were lying
without skin or blood.
Lying like fragmented ashes
to cover our wounds.

The graves
seem to go on forever.

But the one I now dig
is not like the others,
not shallow,
not easily uprooted
not ready to squander its own tombstone.

But,
not all the dead have final resting places.
Those are yet decaying above ground,
arms raised for another revelation
found throughout the earth.

Thunderstorm Art

I have always admired day-storms.
It was as if God had taken the time out
to paint across the sky
on the dark purple canvas.

The people—*scattered!*—
moved out of the way
in white holiness.
And all the colorful
cotton-candy clouds
as twisted strokes
squeezed out
the Fury of Lightning!
Explosive,
it was spilled blue-white paint
dripping down
but always quickly cleaned.

And a tear from the canvas,
heard throughout the heavens,
proceeded by a million small droplets falling,
scattered like kamikazes dying in the wind,
exploding with dead colors,
delivering us the very thing
we try to cover so much.

Waking up

My dream ends!

It's that simple.
I wake up.
It's morning.
The sunlight cutting through my window
blinds my eyes.
The alarm going off
startles me out of sleep.

It takes me five minutes to move,
to pull the covers off my body
and go into the kitchen
to get a nice, good cup of coffee.

The sunlight still invades
picking up dust
from the floor
while I drink as slow as I can.

I am almost 25 years old—
these things should not disturb me
like they do.
But I keep hearing the footsteps
of the man in my dream,
going up and down
the sidewalk.

I think I see him,
but I won't open that door,
I won't unlock it.
I think of escaping through the back,
throwing myself out into the busy streets,
hoping to get lost in the maze of it all.

But I do not leave.
I remain trapped in my house,
hoping that changing the locks
will keep this dark stranger away.

Yggdrasil's[1] Ashes

There was a small article
in the local newspaper,
front page,
telling of my grandparent's house
burning to the ground.
I had seen it printed the next day.

Strange,
how nothing of true value was mentioned,
how they didn't even say that my grandparents
had lived there for over forty years
sitting directly across from City Hall.

---

1 Yggdras-il. In Norse Mythology, a gigantic ash tree which gave
support to the entire universe and was to finally be destroyed at
the end of time. It has roots extending to Niflheim (the
Netherworld), Jothunheim (home of the Giants), Midgard
(Earth), and Asgard (home of the gods).

I still remember, quiet vividly,
how we could always gather
walking those now crisp halls.

There were pictures in the rooms,
tiny souvenirs placed on shelves
that we can never find anymore.

I look towards
where the building once stood,
the frame now ash.

Sometimes I think
City Hall,
the Fire Station, the park
all across the street,
all burned up that night too.
I can remember going to sleep,
hearing cars race
and remember exactly how it sounded,
how the lights overlapped the windows.

It's not like that at their new home.
It is in a different city—
there is no City Hall across the street,
no Fire Station, no park,
no cars racing at the front porch.
Maybe the yard

is too big to hear it,
but I think it is also
because there aren't that many of them
anymore.

It has been years since that fire took the home,
but it still haunts me that I will never see
the largest picture in that house—
the one hanging in the front room
having all the grandchildren collected some
fifteen years ago.
I will never see memories from the
'84 World's Fair in New Orleans.
Never see the Grand Canyon,
the Silverton-Durango train,
Stone Mountain,
the old-timey telephones
placed on the wall.

I could never understand
how it came down so fast.
I was just there a few weeks before
for Christmas.

That house was a quilt made of the same cloth
my mother used, collecting so many images
sown in the one on the first bed

that was burned when that bedroom
went up in smoke.

No,
I don't think
that fire,
ever stop burning.

I have these memories,
these secrets trapped inside me
ticking away like a ship being
sent to all the undiscovered countries
of the world.

And Yggdrasil's Ashes are scattered,
the world having ended.
Yet I will remember
and the wind will blow itself back to me.

Far Beyond the Stars

The evening overshadows me.
At my home,
it becomes strangely comforting:
a song coming as cool as the breeze.

I cannot be the painter.
I can only look at the sparkle shining
at the opposing window,
lying in pale moonlight.
I can only dream of all the beautiful colors
coming together but can never form them.

The autumn breeze, now like snow.
I imagine there must be a world falling,
each filled with different faces.
People, sitting back,

seeing the sunrise for the very first time,
somehow dreaming of a place
far beyond their grasp.

In The Tabernacle of the Pines

What sinister night can bark
to the ash-covered moon?

It is an eye cased in bones,
resting above.
It has gazed at me
and wondered of the dust
moving in the mist of trees,
wondered of the tiny snowflakes
drifting clear as glass,
moving from treetop to treetop
in this tabernacle.

The wind sounds with trumpets,
and we drift asleep.
And until the sun cracks the sky,
our campfire gnaws each amber

floating towards dawn,
floating upward
burning all the snowflakes.

To Those that are Dedicated

To my sons and daughters,
to those that are dedicated.

I have searched for one such as you,
praying your hard work would be complete.

Your loyalty is
a Crown of Thorns
you have freely driven
upon your own head.
I cry for your pain,
wanting to wipe every mark clean
as if they never happened.

You let the blood run,
something you could never be
prideful in.

I have wanted to know more about this pain.
I have wanted to make it my own
because you are not always as courageous
or as strong
as others hope.

It is Forgiven
by the strong faith
you have.
I have even learned to take comfort in them,
with the company you are known by.

I struggled at this:
What might I say to you?

I know you though:
you are the final descendents
of the Apostle Peter:
so full of boldness
and so great a potential
but sometimes speaking of foolish things.

All these words previously unspoken
have not slipped from my tongue
after this time.

And I am forever confident
before you leave,
I will see on your face,
a smile that will not end.

Praise

I am dumbfounded,
unable to speak this properly.

It is an art,
carefully crafted over and over
just like any other.
And although it can be inspired
by the noblest of admirations,
I do not know how it is to be formed.

I have heard the words spoken so perfectly.
As if, on the clearest morning,
the sun rose from a clear sky.
The painter made all the even, wide strokes
as he was born to do,
having every color flow together,
giving strength to the eyes
of the observer.

I find I can not always do this.
Sometimes,
my mountains are not quite silenced.

Even in the quiet nights
where there is silent weeping in the heart,
where the night air is powerless to be the serpent
across my skin I want it to be.

How can this art be cut from the hardest stone?
How can it be found in the very heart of the

Earth?
For these hearts are always
frail enough to burn
with each passing ember.

I know I have danced, at times,
on the clouds non-existent.
Yet I always seem to find myself
wanting this art contained,
lassoed like a mighty creature
running wild and free.

If only I could force myself
to burn my hands in the rope
and ride the wind.

Nervosity

This unstill night goes on,
swinging like the axe above me,
back and forth,
tied to the thin string,
missing my neck by only a few inches.
Tick, tock.

I learned this fascination years ago
by a man who, in his drunken fury,
claimed I was as worthless as sand.

One—
Two—
Three—
Four—
Five—

The echoes of
the revolver rotations
go off near my head.

I had always hoped that my brains
       would splatter against the wall
somewhere inbetween,
because I could never do the sixth.

I would wait for it,
pray for it—
but it never did come.

          At last,
          I squeeze the round

only finding it
just as empty
   as the other five.

On a Park Bench, in the Middle of the Night, Dreaming

In the arms of the still night
I rest like a newborn
upon this bench.
Those around me will sleep away.
and I will whisper
"Do not wake now, you dreamers.
The war drums are silent.
No crowds are here.
Nothing but tranquility
as the sun has eased its heavy rod
off our bare backs."
I know this will not always be.

Soon, the sun will crack the sky
and everyone will wake
to find our hearts all shattered.

Old Memories
Reflected
like the Bright Sun

I think there were twelve of them:
hard, glass mugs—
clear like the memory of the old widow
who had owned them.

When she died, my mother was fortunate
enough to collect these relics
to serve as an embodiment of this thought.

I accidentally threw them all away,
thinking they were nothing more than trash
stuffed in a brown paper bag.

So,
upon my sister recommendation,

last Christmas,
I bought new ones for my mother.
And although the old widow has never
touched these in her life,
her memory still shines forth,
reflected like the bright sun.

To a Guitar at Half-Past Three

The tunes were always mellow
like fallen leaves,
dying
at this time of day.
But I see no leaves out here now.

And the sun shines so bright
that it is enough to make a body wish
Death would just stroll into town,
like a Sunset
on the back of a horse.

But Death never comes.
Nor the sunset.
Surely not in *this* town.

The dust just flies in your face
as ol' Benny plays his guitar

at the saloon
wishing his fingers would
burst into flames
as he strums
over and
over and
over again.

(His fingers never catch on,
but he keeps hoping.)

Spearfishing like Death

Every time,
every night that I enter the bay,
the water is always too cold for me.

It is a tradition to come here
once every summer.
This is the fifth in a row
that my dad and I have been
in the midst of thirty strangers
wading knee deep
guided by flashlights.

We do not know where or when
this tradition began.
Yet we are ready to
fish with spears,
quickly positioning ourselves to stab
our targets in half.

And we are forced to travel slowly.
Partially because we must bow
to the pressure of the bay.
Partially because the other fishermen
get so agitated when the fish are scared.

I have always been hesitant to strike;
my aim slightly off,
the fish flee
before the ground is struck.
Perhaps my own body sabotages me.
Believing my foot will be cut,
it shakes my hand just slightly.

By now I am far more interested
in kicking up sand.
I do not come here for the fish.
I come here for the moon and the men,
to watch the moonlight reflecting off the bay,
encompassing everyone of us in pale images.

At times, it has rained.
Sometimes a soft mist,
sometimes a heavy downpour.
But we will never leave,
only when lightning and thunder
reveal our presence to the sky.

Yet I think I like it better when it rains.
as the moon will twist and turn
like bleeding rosebuds.

When I taste the drops,
they are always cold,
dripping to my toes,
causing all the fish around me
to murmur into the night.

Rare Breed

The passion of our pep rallies
could keep time with the hoof beats
prancing across the bleachers.
Each pounding was like a cannon,
firing off at the stroke of victory.
And I can still hear ol' Mr. Falstaff,
high above,
yelling into the night,
swearing that he could hear chimes
going off in his head.

My Reaction to Stress

Knowing that I am late
for an important meeting with friends,
I travel through this wooden area
faster than I should.
My heart races
when I see the blue flashing lights
in my rear view mirror.
I slow down and pull over to the side of the road.

"Stay calm," I tell myself,
for all the good it will do.

The officer comes to my window
and asks me if I knew that it would
cost me $150
for the speeding I just did.

"Aaaaaaaaaagggh!" I scream in reply
slamming my head on the steering wheel relent

lessly.
The officer takes two steps back from my car,
not knowing whether he should take me into cus

tody
or run for his life.

He instead decides to put his hand on his pistol,
carefully watching my every move.
"Are you all right?" he finally asks.

"I'm fine," I reply as I stop pounding my head.
(Actually, that is a small, white lie
for I am suffering from a massive headache).

I look into his eyes,
and for some reason,
I feel that he doubts my sincerity.

Paint Me
Colors Like the Rain

Paint me colors like the rain.

Paint me blue like waters rushing in.

Paint me brown, red, and orange
like the earth decaying,
sliding out before me.

Paint me green,
like the grass of the field I roll in,
scratching away at every dry itch.

Paint me black as sin
eating my dead body,
baked in the sun.

Paint me all the colors of the rain.
Paint me

like the blood-red dance
dripping from my arms.

But above all,
paint me white like the wind,
constantly and methodically
flying me away.

Standing in Front of the Mirror

Standing in front of the mirror,
as the steam from the shower passes through,
he looks at the other side,
wiping away the blurred images.

His shoulders back,
head up,
chest out.

"No!"
He stops,
Too much vanity
is not a good thing.

His weak form slouches
(but never too much),
his eyes squints

trying to see all better.
But he never does.
Not here like this.

He smacks his lips,
carefully considering his next pose.
Then quickly,
as if he should have known all along,
he rubs his chin
with thumb and forefinger,
pretending to be a scholar.
("Maybe I should shave,"
he tells himself,
"this half-beard is tickling my face.")

As the fog sneaks in
to distort his image,
he cleans it,
before jokingly doing a quick flex,
trying to impress no one,
not even himself.

He leans forward
trying to get a better view of himself,
the fog only standing in the way.

(god) of the People

Wearing the mark for years,
it has become my tourniquet:
keeping my arm attached
to the rest of my body.

I do not want to take it off.
I do not want to be cast aside
in front of these people.

It would be far easier for me
to sacrifice Isaac
since he is already tied down.
It is far easier for me to die
with the mighty statue at my tomb.

I am told this pressure
is too much for me.
It is so great my arm tends
to bleed.

My bones:
old and decaying,
cracking every time the winds blow
against me.

I fight this feeling
for the sake of my godhood.
I know the air is too tight,
and we could all die in an instant,
all bottled up,
as if we were lost at sea,
rocking back and forth on
an endless voyage
before going under.

If we break this bottle now,
we would not drown:
our bodies would rip
into a thousand pieces beforehand.

Soon, in this dark,
I will hear nothing but moaning,
see nothing past my eyes,
except for the few candles
slowly burning,
disappearing from my view.

The Waiting

All the stones were lined up
perfectly in a circle out in the open field
surrounded by trees no more than a hundred feet away.

We sat waiting for something to happen.
For God,
for UFOs,
Maybe for the comet that was going to doom us all.
Anything!

But there were no sounds
other than the burning campfire
and the wind soaring through the trees.

We never moved from that place,
always waiting in the dark,
quietly praying to be moved.

The Canary at
the Twelve O'clock Hour

There is an old church cellar
made centuries ago
that has not been visited in ages.
And for a good reason, I'm sure.

I used to look at its small, broken window
only reflecting the outside world,
until one night
a canary,
(of all things)
flew inside.

I have wondered what was found.
None others of the outside world could go there.
Were there old church records
of who was born, who died,
of who was married, and sermons trapped away?

I never saw that bird come out,
never saw it bring the olive branch
that the dove brought Noah,
always wondering
if it ever found its place to rest
inside that cold cellar.

Eulogy

I walked into our room,
half-expecting you to be there
waiting for me.

Nothing changed,
Except you were not there.

Our departure was violent enough
to make the Red Sea seem as pathetic as a stream.
(Yet, as we know,
Pharaoh's army still traveled through,
not fearing the death that could
(and did) so easily come).

This place seems so much like an altar
for pagan worship.
I don't even know why I entered
in the first place.

Could I ever be Lazarus?
Could I ever rise from this dead,
seeing you
as if for the first time?

Sophisticated Quills

I found my neighbors,
The Jacksons,
to be strange,
always writing with feathers
as a piece of life
that just would not die.

Perhaps because they were old
was why they used them.
I do not know if the family wore wigs,
or only read hardcover books
because I never saw them.

I know the study in their house
was perfectly visible through the windows.
And the desk in the center
was made of solid oak.
I had seen these things millions of times.

I could swear those books
on the shelves were rotting away.
The quills mysteriously remained,
dripping ink, I'm sure, with every third letter,
scraping the paper,
falling like dead trees.

Airplane Downing

The pilot reports to the control tower
both engines have failed.
From 100,000 feet in the air,
the airplane descends
to all the waiting city below.

As they come faster,
pushing aside the beautiful pink clouds,
the stewardesses only pour coffee and cream
into styrofoam cups
to jolt sleeping brains
with caffeine.

Falling,
in the cockpit,
the pilot and co-pilot begin to play
with all the controls,
finding which ones still work and

which ones don't.
(Oops! There went all the luggage.
The clouds are now raining
underwear and hiking gear.)

The elderly quietly
read books and work crossword puzzles,
falling asleep as lullabies
softly play in their headphones,
unable to be helped
with the coffee.

And as they come
to the full runaway, filled with a crowd,
all gathered and holding signs of
"Welcome Home!" and "We Love You!"
the plane hits,
slides,
and bursts into flames.
The crowd, burning like a forest,
where no one can ever survive.

Abba, Father

I have whispered all the common names
of familiarity
over and over again.
I try to ease myself,
only being partially successful.

I learned that I am not the son
of the people who birthed me.
We are not alike in what we eat,
what we drink,
where we lie down to rest.
I have been recarried for another nine months,
growing a different face.

My bones are dry
as all these walls are strong and secure,

built from bridges long since torn down,
not finding a way for the paths
to ever come together again.

With Each Gentle Breeze

With each gentle breeze
they die,
carried away like leaves to a naked field.

It has not rained here
in some time:
the ponds have long since
dried up.
It is now like a desert—
with trees dead,
thirsty, rotting away at their roots,
trying to contain their children
nestled within their branches,
but they could not.
Nothing could stop them
from flying out in their own time.

And now the wind carries them
as a new mother,
as far as they can go
before they crumble,
falling deep within the dusty cracks
breaking open at the surface.

Poeting

I sit

     Remembering all the cold Decembers
     (back when it was cold),
     praying for snow.
But that's the way it is:
we wait
      because there is no more snow in Florida.

  We make our   heavens
  out   of   clay
      but   there   is
      never any   snow.

The Boy in the Yellow Sun

I know nature was not meant
to look upon the sun,
not to understand all its glory.

And the light will blind me,
touching the back of my sockets,
causing me to shut my eyes
phasing in and out.

But I will
gaze at the heavens
looking for that boy, I hear,
trapped inside.

Rain for Dead Flowers

It has been so hot and dry lately
not even flowers can live.

It has been like this for months now:
the heavens silent in their calling,
closed up, giving no comfort,
having nothing but blue days and blistering suns.

The soil is as glass
with cracked lines everywhere.

And when the rain finally does come,
the flowers, being perished,
have stretched out their life
long after their time
trying to rise up
in a previous defiance.

And with each drop
that falls,
the plants are forever broken
falling into shallow tombs
incapable of containing them.

Whitewashed Tombs

No,
We are not like that!

We are bold,
Strong as rocks,
Intelligent as scholars!

We are not cold and lifeless
Like bones in a tomb.
We are not!

You say
"We are as powerless as the air."
But even the wind can
Knock down trees,

You think
We are monsters,
Creatures of the night

With hideous fangs and wild hair,
Eating children before you.

And although we can sometimes find
the Dust of Dead Men intoxicating,
We are never these Whitewashed Tombs,
Rotting and decaying,
As you claim.

Anonymous

Sitting alone,
lost in the dark corner,
all 225 lbs. of him
watches the dance spin like a revolver
pointed at the dark part of his brain.

The flavor slowly dissolves
in his mouth.
But he does not dare leave this place;
the dance is not over yet.

Color the Moon

The moon is so bleak,
a rock white as Death's face.

So Color the Moon!
Paint it rising above the dark night!

Color it with your crayons:
yellow,
green,
red,
and blue.
(Black, if you dare.)

Color it
as your paintings,
your peoples.
Let it shine.

Go out.
Run into the night.
Go,
Color the Moon.

Writing You
Once More for Luck

It has been so long
since I've heard from you.
There has been no letter
in my mailbox,
no phone message
on my answering machine.
Have you all but forgotten
I am still alive?

At times, it makes me think
that you use these letters
nothing more than firepaper.
(I hope you do not.)

We all still think of you,
from time to time,

more apparent than
the statues at City Hall
even though you are not
among them.

We never speak,
but I can see these things
in our eyes.
And at times,
it makes me believe
this town vacant
filled only with the dead.

We are ready for you
to ride right back into this place
as if your departure was nothing more
than a bad tale to scare the drunks with.

In the Land of the Living

she doesn't want to think about it.
and it is somewhat difficult
for me to tell her
as her hands are shriveling up
and she is no longer as young
as she was yesterday.

she knows
that it is only a matter of time
before she rests on the other side
of the tombstones.
although she says
she has believed for a long time
that this will not be the end,
that there is a far better life
awaiting,
she is nervous about this one's close.

it was different
when these things were untouchable
as the cuban air.

it was different when only
older people died.

i cannot live to tell what its like to not to breathe,
how it feels to pass from one reality
to the next.
i want to,
as if i had some acute knowledge
about the subject,
but i don't.

we walk silently,
both thinking
but none saying a word.

she finally breaks the silence
with all her thoughts:
of traveling,
of visiting old friends,
of working long hours in the garden.
she speaks of doing this
as if she was twenty years younger,
but everyone knows she is not.

i want to tell her to be reasonable,
but i don't want to press this subject.

instead, she hides in the forest
and never speaks
of the dark tomorrows coming.

Cabbage

I despise cabbage.
Always have.

As a child,
I remember my mother
would all but force it down my throat,
spoonful by spoonful.

She said I had to eat a scoop
(more like a mountain).
The thought caused nightmares
of not getting to your glass fast enough.
Every time, my meal would last
for twenty or thirty minutes past everyone else's.
Finally (thank God!) my father had had enough
and told her that
"Everyone has their likes and dislikes with food."

But it was evil. (dagnabit!)
Evil!

So if you see me out there,
later on in life,
slinging cabbage on mother's grave,
please remind me that
I am wasting all the good fertilizer.

Because I Must Say Goodbye

There are times
I wish I could go back
and do it all over again.
I was thankful everyday,
several times throughout,
but this did not seem to be enough.

I never said "goodbye" to you after this,
never opened my mouth to say
all the things I should have
when all the things I didn't want happened.

I hoped until the very end it would not.
I was surer than blood
passing through my veins
that it would not.

I know you saw the sun rise.
I only pray that it has not
quickly set in your presence.

Maybe I do not see
when I am gone.
Maybe
my mind is
scattered unto the wind.

I have thought of God and you often,
two intermixed in one thought.

At your time,
you were to ride out
and make kings envious of your name.

I hope only to shine your horse's shoes,
if nothing, but for one day more.
Or for me,
in these feeble clothes,
to anoint your head with the same oil
that came to the ones
before you.

Rise/Set

He opens his eyes before the sun
just to witness
the light shooting across the horizon.

On this hill,
on this beach,
he lets the soothing sands
rush through his fingers
as if trying to hold every one of them.
As if by grabbing them,
he can force the crashing waves
from pouring in like sledgehammers,
raping the soft, sweet shore.

Later on,
in the crowds, he leaves
only to return and see
the passing sun resting over the ocean

under the sky.
And he will once again feel
the cooling sands drifting through.

The Other ByPass

I finally regain consciousness
in the recovery room.

I am alone here
as none of the doctors
or nurses
or family members
decided to wait.

The surgery seems to be a success
as far as I can tell
from these first few moments.

I know I shouldn't be doing this,
but I stand up;
I just have this aching need
to get to my feet.

I notice I have no I.V.,
which I think is really strange,
but I let it pass.

Glancing around the room,
it takes me a little while to focus.
My gaze finally rests on
a large red knot.

I know it is not just any knot.

I quickly place my hand
on the center of my chest
to find no pulse:
And I know that
that shrew has ripped my heart
clean out.
The thought is enough
to cause me to miss a beat
if I even had one.

I stare at it there on the table.
wanting to puke,
wanting to throw my guts out,
but that is liable to only make matters worse.

It's still beating—
that stupid thing,

just pumping air now.

I'm feel so weak at the knees,
I collapse.
And as I begin to phase out again,
I know
that with the rising cost of health care,
she's liable to charge me double
for just dying here.

Zooming By

My younger cousin turned his corners
at 45, 50 miles per hour,
and traveled down his streets
between 60 and 70
as the two of us were
in his white sports car.
He was surely out to parade
his ability to drive
to both me and the world.
I'm impressed! I'm impressed!,
I thought,
(More like scared half out of my mind!)
But my silence,
my secret swearing in my mind,
my worried eyes
were not enough
to slow him down.

He probably wasn't even looking at me,
which was fine as long
as he kept his eyes
on the road.

Trying to make idle conversation,
he couldn't distract me from seeing all the

houses zoom by.
Maybe some bourbon would be nice
–for me, not for him!
I remember thanking God
no one was on
those streets that day.

We stayed on course,
unchanged,
turning in and out,
going over one hill,
and down the next,
racing as if we were already late for something,
but had all the time in the world
and no place to go.
I began breathing heavily, trying to store up

enough air
just in case if we hit something, I would sur

vive.
Somehow.
We slowed down, briefly,
to see new houses being built,
and I relaxed.
But soon it was time to head back
the way we came in,
how we came in:
mentally swearing,
moving recklessly,
desiring a drink,
keeping my mouth shut,
watching,
fearing,
breathing,
and praying.

The Greatest Monument

There is a particular statue I love—
its craftsmanship impossible to be denied—
standing graceful in its own right
at the museum in town
on the hard floor.

I do not know of who's image it is,
only that it is strong,
fully clothed with beard.

I have never seen one so smooth.
There is usually a slight imperfection typically done.
But there is not even a
small, uneven crevice upon the body.
Fingerprints are upon the hands
as if blood could pass through.

What is seen is good,
but *how* it is seen is better.
All the light,
from every direction,
shines upon this one,
producing no shadows.

How many years,
how many decades,
was necessary
to do this,
going over and over,
a sculptor chipping away
all the pieces so callously defined?

When I Pray to the God of Heaven

I used to stop and pray on a hillside
where a large cross was planted.
There,
putting rose petals at the feet,
I would say my piece
before going into town.

It was a year later,
when I was told someone was buried there,
I felt robbed of all my experiences,
making them less grander than belief.

I don't plant rose petals at that cross anymore.
I don't even pray there.
Maybe I should.
Maybe some dead person lying there

shouldn't bother me,
but it does.

I now go to the church in town,
enjoying the music
being played in the next room
for next Sunday.
I pray for an hour at a time—
longer than I used to do at the gravesite.
And during this time alone,
I never force myself
to look up and see the candles flickering,
moving back and forth
pushed by the wind entering through the window.

Our Tree

As children,
playing high above the earth,
we nestled ourselves at the highest
point and shook the branches back
and forth, watching the
leaves fall helplessly to the
ground. But one day, we shook
those branches
and   lost
our
balance.   Falling   ,
one
by one,   help-   less-   ly
spinning   out of
control.   Descending
to the   big pile, ready to be buried.

The Heartless Express

There is a train,
speeding into the night,
a bullet-shot phantom,
roaring with stream,
turning its wheels past us all,
slowing down for no one.

I want to call it
"The Heartless Express"
over its cold, hard expressions
and soot-covered sides.
The smoke from the chimney
is spewed like a demon
filled with the remains of the earth,
covering the front dim light
like a dusty pearl thrown by slingshot
soaring through all outdoors.

They say it is cold onboard—
bitingly cold!—
as there is no room for blankets
on the stiff, leather seats.
And all the heat is forced upward
through the pipes
as the cranks and levers turn
and send the train on its way.

I do not know
its real name.
I do not know
where it is ever going
or who it is caring.
But I hear many will pay
all they have to stay onboard,
to move so fast
that not even the beaten tracks
can be heard below.

Giving Thanks

It has been years
since I have eaten
that dry, crusty bread.
I can still remember my mother
buttering it for me,
hidden in the streets,
with some lost metal,
always covering
the normalness of this life.

Even the Small

I have noticed that
even small bees are enticed
by large flowers.
There is just something
about their fragrance
when they are standing before them.

Once,
one particular speak of a bee was hovering
ever-so-slightly
above such a flower.
Landing in that soft bed of yellow,
the bee pushed its legs upward, back and forth,
its tiny needles scraping the face.

Its intent could never be hidden:
small leaps were made,
pushing away strand by strand.

Within an hour
the plant was gone,
completely withered up and dead.
I never thought this bee
was capable of a tragedy.
I don't know how it hid everything
it stole being as small as it was.

Yet it still managed to take off,
drifting,
drunk in its success,
slowly returning to the hive.

Before Fading as a Phantom

Tonight,
the fog drifts like clouds
over the moon,
largely threatening to rain.

And when I begin
to feel the soft mist,
I can still see clearly enough.

There!
Floating through the tombstones
is a form
I never make out,
but it is enough for me
to follow.

The caskets beneath
rattle a consecutive moan,

longing for this mysterious phantom:
longing for that which they can never touch.

I, too, am hunting,
running through dark graveyards,
praying that the rain does not come down harder,
impounding the mystery past life,
hoping that the sun will wait
one more hour before rising
so I may see this thing
face-to-face.

I fear I never will—
I will never be closer
than I am now.
Only running,
searching,
until I lie in my grave.

I Knew You Before Your Time

I remember when my son died,
killed in a car accident,
his broken body laying crushed
still in his mother's womb.
The other driver,
although drunk that night,
was not charged with murder.
My child,
waiting to be declared "legally alive."

We still have the baby furniture
in the other room,
baby toys,
unplayed with.
The mobile
just hanging over the crib.

This house feels empty,
as if something,
someone,
should be running through the halls,
knocking over lampstands
tracking mud over
the newly-vacuumed carpet.

I remember Monday it rained,
and I thought I saw a familiar face
running with yellow jacket and galoshes
through mudpuddles, jumping up and down.
But it was no one I knew,
no one in particular.

Sometimes I will wake
from a pseudo-prodigious sleep,
swearing I can see him
in that room I am
so afraid to enter.

I knew him—
my son—
before his time,
before he could open his eyes
and watch television for the first time;
before he could read his first book;

before he could go on the fishing trips
that will remain forever unexplored.

I think of all the things
that might have been.
And I wonder
what would his life have been like
had I never known him?
Could his boyish smiles ever stop me
from hearing the rain
drip out in front of the sun?

Leaving Town

As night comes,
you prepare to depart
from the bus station.

It is exactly 5:15 p.m.
You've got your life.
I've got mine.
We keep trying to tell each other that,
trying to believe.

I feel that this is the end to
more than one thing,
more than one life.
The sun is slowly setting.
Right now it is where
it can blind us
before passing over to the horizon.

There is a lot of noise in the background,
but there is just silence between the two of us.
I can think of nothing
but the bus pulling in,
and how I wish
it could stay longer.

It doesn't.
You're onboard and it leaves.
And even I know that that bus
would run me over
if I ever tried to stop it.

Taming the Dark Night

Saturday morning.
1 a.m.

I stand on the corner of Jackson
and Fifth
with a few of friends I brought
for company.

Every place seems to breathe
with a Rhythm.
We hear it outside,
and we do know that how
the neighbors sleep
in a time like this.

The city lights are dim,
but the banners and open windows
are more than enough for us to find our way.

We think about going inside one particular place,
removing ourselves from the shadows.
But we know,
sometimes it is better just to watch,
to smell the savored wine
but never taste.

When we do go in,
the crowd gives no more room
as it dances
and talks,
and does God-only-knows-what.

After we dance,
we fall to the floor,
our bodies too used up
after the songs end.

By sunrise, with our bodies sore,
we manage to get up and walk away.
Stepping over every person,
we ache with every slight movement,
but we all manage to get up
and walk away.

The Journey
Has Never Ended

Sometimes
I walk for miles
stopping at trees,
staring until I can
see my reflection
gazing back.

Sometimes
I have drowned a creek
by shooting out like a cannonball,
drifting down stream.

Sometimes
I will gaze at the sun,
waiting for the stars to come out.

But often,
I will just run after the leaves
twisting in the night air,
chasing comets with wooden sticks,
trying to catch the stars,
only to feel them burn in my hands
while the dry, dusty rocks
stab my bare feet.

About the Author

Jay Gallops was born on July 16, 1974 in Metarie, LA, outside of New Orleans. He grew up (and current lives) in Pensacola, FL were he has recently served as an editor to Pensacola Junior College's literary journal, *Half Tones to Jubilee.*

www.ingramcontent.com/pod-product-compliance
Lightning Source LLC
Chambersburg PA
CBHW031304060726
47590CB00003B/1056